You Were the Music

You Were the Music

Barb Shadow

From the Shadows Publishing
Livingston Manor, New York

To those you left behind . . .
And to the ones who greeted you
On the other side

Red Thread

They say that there is a soulmate out there in the world for everyone and we are connected by a red thread. It's tied to our fingers and, eventually, we will come together. I would love to believe this, and I hope it's true.

I'm starting to lose faith that I will find my soulmate in my life. Maybe I'm meant to be alone . . . I know the thread is invisible, but it would be nice to look down and see it tied to your hand . . . and be able to follow it.

They say there's someone for everyone, but what if I never meet them in my lifetime? Will I meet them in another life?

Or are they right in front of me? I don't think so, or I would know it. Would love to follow it and be led to a pretty hand.

Sometimes it's a lonely life and I would love to have someone to share it with. She's out there . . . I know she is. I just have to be patient and have faith. Maybe this year will be the year.

I will know when I look in her eyes if she's the one for me.
.

Darren Steele

Three years before we met

You know you're at your lowest
when the poetry begins

Death

The word is foreign
On my lips
Yet too familiar

When one tear falls
A thousand more
Follow

Wednesday

My phone keeps ringing
The care team updates us
And then oncology calls

My thoughts are a tornado
But words stab through

Aggressive
Multiple organ failure
Too fragile to move to hospice
Palliative care

Final hours

Final

Hours

Emptiness

There is a gaping hollow
Within me
That pulls the oxygen
From my lungs

My hands shake

Thursday

Thursday
June 27

1:14 pm

My phone rings

The doctor says
You passed at 1:10

And do we want an autopsy

Cancer is an insidious bitch.

We Didn't Talk About Cancer

In between doctors' visits
We didn't talk about cancer
We set our sights on the stars
Getting a little place
On the Mediterranean
And drinking wine
Having champagne
Atop the Eiffel Tower
And the grandchildren we'd have
We didn't talk about cancer

In between chemotherapy appointments
We didn't talk about cancer
Or when we sat in the corner of the room
While the chemo dripped
Laughing and joking, teasing each other,
Until you looked at the nurses and said,
"We're always like this. It's how we are!"
But we didn't talk about cancer

In between hospital stays
We didn't talk about cancer
Two-hour drives to the city
Four weeks spent on the oncology floor
Bringing you cards and fresh shirts
A pirate eyepatch
To fool the double vision
So you could read my text messages
And send me hearts

We didn't talk about cancer

Even when you came home for a week
And I helped you from bed
To the bathroom
To the couch
We didn't talk about cancer

You longed for the energy
To play guitar
Build onto our home
Show me Italy
And I said,
"Soon.
It's on the horizon.
Just sail your ship toward it."
And you would answer,
"I hope so."
We clung to hope
And I believed
But we didn't talk about cancer

As confusion settled into your mind
And weakness your body
We didn't talk about cancer
You'd call to tell me Indy car drivers
Had visited the hospital
Stopped in your room
And chatted a while
I couldn't tell if it was real
But you believed it
They didn't talk about cancer

And when you called that Sunday
Unsure of where you were
And I said,

"Honey.
You're in the hospital."
You told me, "I'm not."
I said, "Okay."
Because where you were was better
Than a sterile room
With IV bags and bedpans
I told you I loved you
On that final call
But we didn't talk about cancer

Lost

I never believed I'd lose you

But that's not true . . .

When you first spoke the words
Multiple myeloma
I was afraid
Read all I could
And dreaded the inevitable
But I pushed that aside
With all my might
To live each moment
As if we had forever

And I convinced myself
We did

I never expected to lose you
And I am lost

The Little Black Ring Box

Medical transport
Drove you to the city
The quickest we could find
On such short notice
You were admitted
To the hospital
Again

And everyone went home

I picked up
Made the bed
And found a little black ring box
On its side
Underneath

We'd moved so many things
Packed boxes
So that when the carpet was laid
And the bed delivered
We could unpack everything
Together
Move in my belongings
And merge our worlds

I tucked it onto the shelf
Of your nightstand
Thinking maybe it was a keepsake
A remembrance
That had fallen out of a larger box

But you didn't come home
Our future crumbled

And when your sister called
She was afraid
It had been lost
The little black ring box
With your mother's ring inside
That you had asked her for
So you could propose

I told her I'd found it
And cried
As if my soul
Had broken

The "What Ifs" are Mind Killers

What if

>You never had myeloma
>Or a stem cell transplant
>And seven years of chemo

What if

>The cancer hadn't compressed your spine
>Hadn't broken your arm

What if

>They started treatment after the PET scan
>There was no double vision
>You skipped the neurologist and beelined to the oncologist

What if

>You hadn't fractured the other arm
>They gave you radiation sooner
>The pneumonia held off
>The C-diff never happened
>Or the diverticulitis

What if

>They found the source of the fevers sooner
>>And the clinical trial began

What if

>I had you here beside me

What if

Crashing of the Waves

I am the shore
Your death
The ocean
The tide moves out
And erodes me
I recover slowly
The sun offers comfort
But there's nothing
It can do
To stop the cycle
Of pain
That returns
Relentlessly
In waves

Never Ending

I wanted to cry today
Felt it through my being
In my bones
And glanced
At the calendar

Thursday

It's Thursday
Again
And just as December
Became a marker for Mom
November, Dad
Thursdays
Are a forever reminder
A weekly mourning
Of when you left
This earth

I Will Never Forget

I am filled with memories
But living
Quiet hours
Sad smiles
And emptiness

I play videos
Of you
On my phone
Short memories
Glimpses
Of the time we shared
And I savor them
For dear life

Sad Moment Caught in Time

The week between hospital stays
It was so good to have you home
Even needing a cane
And support
To get to the bathroom
The couch
The bed

Thirty pounds lighter
A white beard softly growing
Even though you were bald
From the chemo
Your eyes incredibly tired
And their shine
Dulled

We joked
Between your naps
As I tried to get you to eat
Just a little
Sip protein drinks
But it had already been
More than six weeks
Since you'd eaten anything

We laughed a little
And I snuggled beside you
Mindful
Of the arm
You'd broken in a fall
Just five months after

The left one fractured

I gathered your medicine
The little boy in you
Making a face
At the taste
But we were working together
To get you well again
So you could be scheduled
For the clinical trial
That would be lifesaving

We talked of our plans
Building an addition
So we'd have room
For grandchildren to play
And a grand Christmas tree
Italy, Paris
And a love to last
The ages

I took your picture
As you glanced at me
As much of a smile
As you could muster
And when you returned
To Mt. Sinai
I couldn't look at it
Knowing your health
Was gone
Your strength
Stolen
Our future

Barb Shadow

In pieces
I deleted that photo

Six Weeks

It's been six weeks
And one day
A forever ending
A sad beginning
Twisted together
Cutting off my breath

We Were

We were supposed to
Grow old together
Fix up the house
Enjoy our later years

We were supposed to
Put a tiny house
Up on the hill
For your youngest
While my oldest
Bought a house
Just down the road

We were supposed to
Go to concerts
Record your next CD
Hold hands in moonlight
And kiss goodnight

We were supposed to
Celebrate birthdays
And holidays
With all the zeal
Enthusiasm
And boyish twinkle
That never left your eyes

We were supposed to
Cook together
Coconut curry cod
With fresh vegetables

From the garden
You pouring beer
For slugs
Me picking tomatoes

We were supposed to
Watch the leaves fall
And the snow

We were supposed to
Make music
Write books
Live life

We were supposed to
Have more time

Uncharted Territory

I've experienced loss
Mom's been gone
Nine years
Dad seven
But we all expect
To lose parents
And we deal
With that sadness
This grief, however,
Is uncharted
No one says
Be prepared
To lose
The love of your life
No one says
The man
Sleeping beside you
Will suddenly
Be gone
Leaving
An empty bed
A path forward
Alone
No one warns you
Of unfathomable
Grief
And disbelief

Dulled

I'm so tired
Of emptiness

The world is distant
And muffled

I crave
The sound of your voice

To make everything
Clear again

Breathe

I am the overthinker
The worrier
Queen of Anxiety
And the first thing you'd tell me
Every time
Was breathe

Breathe

Always your solution
To every bump
In the road
Nothing was impossible
Nothing irreparable
Everything would be
Okay

Breathe

Who will remind me
To take a step back
Be calm
Now that my world
Has crashed
Who will tell me
To breathe
When everything
Inside me
Is a silent scream

Sunglasses and a Smile

I miss your hand
Resting on my thigh
As I drive

Time

Time passes differently now
Slowed
Twenty-three hours since you passed

Three days

Six weeks

Your death is a pinpoint
In my reality

Forty-six days

And I have felt every one of those
One thousand one hundred four hours

Every day mocks me
As the weeks slide
Out of my grasp

Finality

When I was a child
I found the concept
Of lasts
Fascinating
That we would all
Do something
For the last time
And never know it
The last bite
Of a cupcake
Last rainy day
Last fish
Pulled from the lake
Or last piece of wood
Tossed onto a campfire
Last book read
Last salmon
In the smokehouse
Last step
Through the front door
Last ride
Last kiss
I'm no longer
A child

Seasons Lost

Summer didn't come this year
It got tangled in hospital stays
And IV bags
Got lost in ten story buildings
And doctors' faces
Phone calls

Summer didn't come this year
There were no tomato plants
Or rollercoaster rides
Just chemotherapy
And tears

Summer didn't come this year
We had a huge get-together
Family and friends
Music and food
100 people came
And called it
A Celebration of Life
When what they meant was
A final farewell
A funeral
Goodbye

Summer didn't come this year
And I don't know
If fall will, either

How do you rebuild when all the bricks are broken?

The Month of Not Caring

We dubbed it
The "month of not caring"
Watched endless hours
Of old movies
Not really seeing
Ate ice cream for dinner
Ordered takeout
Three times a day
It didn't matter
We didn't care
I'm not even sure
I got dressed
Much
What else can you do
When you're punched in the gut
And your heart
Lies beating on the floor
Not knowing
If it will recover
Or find its way back
Into your chest
In one piece

Sorry
I'm too sad
To be poetic

Our Bethlehem

I stood in our bedroom
This morning
The lavender walls
Failing to soothe
I found myself
Staring
At the Moravian star
Hanging on the wall
Beside the bed

We found that star
With its purple glass points
On one of our trips
To Bethlehem, PA
Your favorite place
With its little shops
And God's Acres

We stayed
In a hotel
Off the beaten path
And walked the city
Stopping at
Grandpa Joe's Candy Shop
Bookstores and
"Witchy" shops
As you called them
Lunch at the Brew Works
You in bliss
Over maple bacon
Brussels sprouts

Already with reservations
At The Sun Inn
For dinner
Taking in its history
And ghosts
Over a glass of wine
In love with life
And each other

Nothing better

I don't know
If I can ever go
To Bethlehem
Again
Without you
By my side

Alone

I crawl into bed
Grab my book
And read
Until I catch it
Falling
From my hands
I roll over
Pull the pillows close
And drape my arm
Across them
Realizing
It's how I laid
Against your back
With my arm
Resting on your thigh
And I miss
Us

Maybe Next Year

The pot of mini roses
Has toppled over
Or maybe it had weeks ago
I know it's been a while
The buds are brown
Dried
Dead

I stand at the door
Staring down at the pot
Thinking
"We must've had wind
last night"
And
"I should go
straighten it"
But so many things
Remain undone

Last summer
My roses grew
Unfettered
Strong
And beautiful
You were here

I don't have the energy
Now
For flowers

43

Everything Has Changed

Don't tell me grief is a process
Or that he's in a better place
That it'll take time
And I'll be okay
Don't
Because I'll never be okay
And I'll never stop missing him
It will always hurt
And my life will never be the same

We Never Lost Hope

A friend of mine
Had multiple myeloma
Another writer
We'd chat here and there
A kind word
Updates
On our book releases
And life

I never mentioned
When he said
That his Revlimid
Stopped working
Or when his wife
Messaged to say
He'd passed
I never told you
He died
Or of the dread
It drilled into me

When your Revlimid
Stopped working
I hoped against hope

Yet here we are
In tears

So Hard

When did life get so complicated
So difficult
When did reality creep in
And announce itself
With a sledgehammer

Hershey Park

We took your youngest
To Hershey Park
For a day of rides
Food and fun
A mini vacation
To shake away
The day-to-day stresses
Of custody battles
And cancer
To be carefree
For a little while
And let the coasters
Be the only reason
For yelling
Your little daredevil
Who backed off
From rides
You yearned for
Stood beside me
To take pictures
As you zoomed by
Crazy thrills
Fueling
Your adventurous side
And your boyish
Excitement
We arrived at our room
With smiles
And exhaustion
As the two of you
Donned bathing suits

Barb Shadow

And ran for the
Hotel pool
With talk of returning
Next year
This year
But summer
Is over now

Stolen Time, Stolen Life

Grief has a funny way
Of stealing time
The month of not caring
The summer that wasn't
Fall nearly here
And I can't

The leaves are changing
Reds and yellows
But grief has turned them
Muddy brown

Day 58

Dreary
Chilly
Fall is here
The leaves are changing
The world
Moves on
Without you

Without me

I need to remember

> To drink water
> That I am not alone
> The sun continues to rise

They tell me

> That someday the weight on my heart will lessen

. . . but I don't believe it

A Love for the Ages

Some scientists say
There are parallel universes
Alternate realities
Infinities

Somewhere
There is a you
Who received CAR T-cell therapy
And beat cancer

Somewhere
There is a you
Who never got cancer

And I know
In every lifetime
We met
And fell in love
Because the love
I have for you
Is greater than
One universe
Can hold

Nothing Feels the Same

I am staring at the calendar
And the long days ahead
Already a blur
A swirling chaos
Of emptiness
We'd shop
And I'd chase you
Through stores
Trying to keep up
And you'd smile
Always zooming along
A man on a mission
Even if it was only to find
The 12' skeleton
In the aisle at Home Depot
So I could marvel
At its glowing eyes
Decorating for Halloween
Thanksgiving
And Christmas
Your favorite holidays
How will I begin to find
A quarter of your
Enthusiasm
When all I can muster
Is sadness

I Miss Your Music

You'd bring out your 12-string
And sing for me
In the living room
I'd lay back
And listen
Alive
With the melodies

You'd debate
Which guitars
To play at your shows
But always bring the 12-string
Because it was my favorite

Now
There is only a sad silence
Where the music
Used to be

Your Adventure

I flipped through
The television guide
And settled on
Old episodes
Of the Amazing Race
As the couples
Dashed from
Country to country
It reminded me
Of your trip
To Europe
Backpacking
With your best friend
Arriving
In a foreign country
With a passport
A list of places
You didn't want to miss
You touched
The Colosseum
And borrowed
A guitar
In Paris
To play
Under the Eiffel Tower
I have the video
Of you singing
It's grainy
With poor audio
But it is grand
You stayed in hostels

And fell in love
With Italy
And France
We made plans
To reach the top
Of the Eiffel Tower
One day
And to tour
The Catacombs

At least
You had
The memories

I Tried

I tried to be productive today
Went to the bank
The pharmacy
Thought about stopping
At Walmart
But forgot
And took the exit home
Decided not to clean
The kitchen
Or sweep
Fold laundry
Pack
But I did wander
Through every room
Ponder
What I could be doing
Then sat on the couch
And did nothing
Got up to use the bathroom
Get a snack
I sat at my desk
And shuffled papers
Thought about writing
Or washing your jacket
But didn't
I've lost so much of you
Already

I hate that you are referred to in past tense.

I Love You, Too

The first time you said you loved me
I was in your kitchen chopping onions
You poured me a glass of wine
Sauvignon Blanc
While the meat defrosted
And we laughed
At my onion-tears
I grabbed the breadcrumbs
You rested your glass on the counter
And leaned against the sink
Arms folded
I glanced over my shoulder
Smiled
And went back to mixing ingredients
You stepped up close
Behind me
And said into my ear,
"I don't think I've ever told you
That I love you . . .
but I do."

And we kissed

What I wouldn't give
To make you dinner
Once more

A Sigh

I think I saw fall
For just a minute
Felt the crisp mist of morning
Soaked in the pale yellows
And oranges
Of leaves still on the trees
And in that moment
Breathed

Day 106

That sounds
Like so much time
And yet it's been hours
Minutes
Since you passed

Three and a half months
It was 37 degrees
This morning
Winter's on the way
But I don't know
Where summer disappeared
Or fall

There's holiday talk
On everyone's lips
Who will host
Thanksgiving
Christmas ideas

My daughter asked
If we could bake
A cake
For your birthday

I said
Of course

But that's not until
Day 176

This is Grief

An endless repetition
Of meaningless tasks
To fill the spaces
Between the hours

I sat on the couch today
Looked
At all that needs doing
Laundry
Dishes
Picking up
The carpet could use
A vacuuming
The kitchen
A sweeping
I sat on the couch
And when the day was done
I was undone

I saw a pot of mini roses
At the store
A pale lavender
So pretty
And brought them home
To cheer myself
A remembrance
Of happier times
I set them outside
On the deck
So the cat
Wouldn't eat them

But when I looked
Out the sliding door
The pot was toppled
Blooms gone
Stems brown
I guess I didn't
Water it

I feel nothing

I have withered

When

When will I write again
When will I be able
To put thoughts onto paper
That aren't
Soul rending
Or end before they start
Mindless distractions
Of video games
Candy Crush
Mass Effect
Diablo
Oblivion
Zuma
Staring at the walls
The television
Endless episodes
Of food competitions
And old sitcoms
I Love Lucy
And Chopped
All from
My sofa
Alone

My creativity is muted
And my muse
Silent

Every time you brought out your guitars, you took my breath away.

Irony

I blasted the radio
In my car
To push out the sadness
How ironic
That thought
Because
You were the music

The Day We Met

I'll never forget
The day we met
You with your brother
On the hottest
August days
Repairing the overhang
On my deck
The wood
Long since rotted
And peeling away
You noticed
Some weak floorboards
And replaced them
To keep me safe
And then
Built a garbage bin
We walked
Up my driveway
Laughing
Chatting
And looking into
Each other's eyes
The work finished
You paused
And said,
"If you're ever in Manor
and, I don't know,
want to grab
a cup of coffee
or something . . .
Call me."

I called . . .
Before you had gotten
A mile down the road

False Hope

I thought I hit
A turning point
For two days
The sun shone
And I noticed
My despair
In the background
My emptiness
A bystander
I could breathe in
The fall air
And exhale hope
Appreciate the leaves
Under my feet

But today
It rained
Forcing leaves
To the ground
Before their time
Stealing
What little life
They had
The dark sky
A weight on my chest

I almost made it

A million years with you would not have been enough.

164 days

Your birthday is this month
Five days before Christmas
Eleven before New Year's Eve
I had always heard
The person you kiss
At midnight
On New Year's Eve
Is who would be
By your side
Throughout the coming year
You believed it, too

I guess last year's kiss
Was a lie
Or perhaps it was
A deeper truth
As you will never leave
My heart

The Romance of the Rain

We'd snuggle
In bed
And listen
To the pouring rain
So safe
So loved
So right
Nowhere else
To be
Together
With the romance
Of the rain

Everything Has Changed

It's six days after Christmas
Lights bright
Presents scattered
The tree still up
Until tomorrow
And the store windows
Are already decorated
For Valentine's Day
It breaks my heart
Deflated
Like a balloon's final landing
In a dusty corner of the floor

The memories flow
Of our first Valentine's together
You made me dinner
Bought chocolate dipped
Strawberries
Little gifts
And for you
I only had a card
Because I hadn't yet realized
I was with a man
Who celebrated every minute
Lived with every breath
Loved
With his soul

I learned quickly
That falling for you
Meant taking your hand

And running on the wind
Valentine's Day is coming
And I
Can barely walk

My days have never held so little meaning.

Six Months Today

I say what's expected
Go where I'm needed
My smiles
Are without feeling
I go through
The motions
Void
A piece of my heart
Left with you
Leaving behind
Something vacant
Abandoned

Half a Year

Six months
Half a year
Half a year
Nothing is easier
Nothing is okay
Six damn months

Remember When

Remember when
We drove to Cooperstown
Just because
It was a getaway
The two of us
Deserving an afternoon
Of wandering
Exploring
We found a restaurant
That had the best
BLTs
And you asked
If they ever had
Live music
We drove
Admiring the sights
And found
An art museum
We went in
On a whim
And spent the afternoon
Going from room to room
Commenting on the sketches
Our girls would like
And in the gift shop
You sold the clerk
Three of my books

On the way home
We stopped
At a small wine shop

And bought a bottle
Of Cabernet Sauvignon
For later that night
With Brie, crackers
And a roaring fire
In the fireplace

How did we
Find love
Just to lose it

Life

I'm lost
With vague anxiety
Sitting in my chest
My mind a blur
Of the undone

Shallow palpitations
Let me know
My heart
Is still beating

Worries

I shoveled today
In old gloves
And your scarf
Threw salt
Across the ice
Careful not to slip
Or hurt my back
Adjusting the gloves
After wiping off
My windshield
There's more snow
On the way
Wednesday
Again
And Saturday
I think about
Last winter
And the ones
Before
You'd have
The snowblower
Tuned up
Oil changed
Topped off
Before the bad weather hit
You had no worries
And now
I have them all

Silence

My phone is quiet
A silent reminder
That you're gone
I never realized
How often we talked
Texted
Messaged
Sent photos
Videos
You were a constant
And now
Your absence
Is

At the Brewery

The hours flow by
And I watch them
Existing in a horrid emptiness

I glance at the photo
We took
At the brewery
The day we got lobster
From the food truck
It was chilly
But you wanted
A picture of us

I stood on line
While you went
To grab a beer
And we shared
A picnic table
With another couple
Musicians like you
And while we ate
Steaming bowls of bisque
You swapped stories
Of performances
And we discussed
My books
Traded phone numbers
Facebook pages
And gig dates
So we could get together

Barb Shadow

It was a wonderful
Afternoon

I wonder what they're doing now

This Has Become My Usual

Tears again
A quiet longing

Why aren't you here
  Why aren't you here
    Why aren't you here
      Why aren't you here with me

I think back to the last time
We were together
You, too tired to open your eyes
Only enough energy
To sleep
Avoiding the pain
And confusion

How did this come to be
I don't understand
I only wish
You were here

Derailed

Grief is a broken train track
Derailing all who travel
Scattering us
Bruised and broken
Leaving us crawling
To search
For a way home

Lasts Have Changed to Firsts

I lived the lasts with you
And didn't know it
Five years gone in an instant
Two months of hospital stays
Nine months since
The chemo stopped working

Our last laughs
Sitting on the couch
Snuggled under blankets
At least you got to sleep
In our new bed
A first and a last
Between trips to Mt. Sinai

Our last kiss
On Tenth Floor, Center
Oncology
You held my face
And kissed me
Once, twice
Three times
And we smiled

My last sight of you
Frail, exhausted
So many IVs
A heart-shaped blanket
Donated for cancer patients
I brought it home
Still with the hope

Barb Shadow

That you'd walk out
A man in remission

But they were lasts

The last clear thoughts
The last infection
The last fever
The last hours
Last breath

And, as hard as they were,
The firsts now leave me
Shattered

Have They Forgotten?

Isn't it funny
How life goes on
The "I'm sorry"
"He's in a better place"
And
"I wish I could help"
Have dwindled
The drop-ins are over
Yet my grief
Continues

You Would Have Loved It

I watched the Super Bowl
Last night
You would have loved it
The game
Hot wings and chips
Your team didn't make it
But neither did mine
You would have loved it
Just the same

Another first
Without you

The Wound May Heal but the Scar Remains

Your death
Bit like a shark
And ripped away
So much of me
In a finality
That I can barely
Comprehend

And I don't believe
I will ever again be
The person I was
With you

You Were the Music

Firey passion
From your head-banging days
Metal running
Through your veins

You were the music

Country roots
Branches of rock
All while writing
Your original blends
Of love gone wrong
And sweaty nights

You were the music

The lights and the stage
Fueling your heartbeat
Filling your lungs
And your lust

You were the music

Solo performing
Open mics
Showcasing your originals
Confident
Yet always
Striving for perfection

You were the music

Light guitar
In the afternoon
Scribbling lyrics
In notebooks
And singing

You were the music

I Sat Today

Watched a movie
Coffee mugs and dirty dishes
Fill the sink
And I know I should
Throw in a load of laundry
The cat box smells
There is mail on my desk
Unopened
And I don't feel like cooking

Grief sucks

The Crickets Still Sing

We listened to crickets
And watched shooting stars
On long, cool nights
Wrapped in sweatshirts
Over pajamas
Leaning back
Tip-worthy
In metal deck chairs
Craning our necks
And breathing in
The crisp night air

I look for you
In the night sky
And listen
For your music
On the breeze
Sipping wine
From a lone glass
While the crickets
Sing

A Second Chance at Life

Today is your
Re-birth birthday
The anniversary
Of the stem cell transplant
That gave us
The years we had

The nurses sang
Happy Birthday
In the hospital
And every year
You relished that date
That gave you
What we thought
Was forever

I thank God
For the time
We had

Maintaining

I have been stagnant
For nearly eight months
At least I
Forwarded my mail
Since the move
To your house
Our house
But I realized
This morning
I have only been
Maintaining
Concentrating
On mindless tasks
Inconsequential
Chores
And minor
Obligations
It nags me
Drives my anxiety
But I will
Get to everything else
Tomorrow

Sadness

One tear
Slides
Along my cheek
Escaping
My defenses
And betraying me

I wipe it away
Pretend I'm okay
But know the dam
Won't hold
Much longer

You'll Always Be My Favorite

I came across the gift
I gave you
Last year
On Valentine's Day
Still tucked inside
Its little box
And I smiled
You had no idea
There'd be a keychain
Inscribed
You're my favorite asshole
Our most used
Term of endearment

All the times we'd joke
Back and forth
Stealing glances
And quietly saying,
"Asshole"
And breaking
Into smiles

You laughed
Totally amused
And kept it
On the coffee table
To show
Every person
Who walked into our home

You Did It for Me

When the snake
Slithered
Into my basement
Doorframe
And stuck its head
Out of the strike plate
I called you
Panicked
Saying
I couldn't leave
The house
You drove thirty miles
To come to my rescue
Only to find
The snake had gone

But you were here

Did I Tell You the One . . .?

I miss the nights
We laughed
Till our ribs ached
Lying in bed
In the dark
You telling joke
After joke
Ridiculous things
But at 2:00 am
Everything
Becomes hilarious
I'd tell you to stop
And you'd say,
"Okay . . .
but have I told you
the one about . . ."
And we'd be rolling
Once again
Kidding
That when you were five
You climbed
Out of your
Bedroom window
Jack Daniels
In one hand
Cigarettes
In the other
To go pick up girls
We'd never laughed
So hard
My ribs

Barb Shadow

Ached
And now it's just
My heart

Grief

Grief has warped time
Made afternoons drag
Nights disappear
It's woken me
At 3:13 am
And 5:00
I watch the clock
The minute hand
Stoic
Yet the hours
Somehow change
Grief has stolen days
And months
I watch
The world around me
People living their lives
Enjoying
Participating
While I, disjointed,
Am a shell
Of a life
Out of time

Winter Storms

I am sad today
A storm is coming
Snow, then ice
We may lose power
But that doesn't
Bother me
Too much
I am ready
The tub is filled
With water
For the toilets
I have salt
For the driveway
And a shovel
It's early morning
And I've had my coffee
English muffin
With cream cheese
But I am low
I put on a movie
Something with
Joan Crawford
Even though
I never liked her
I am sad
But my bills are paid
Spring is coming
So many good things
To look forward to
But I am sad today

Love

I wasn't looking for love
But I found it

Not the love from my teens
Those drama-riddled crushes
Infatuations that filled my heart
Almost to bursting
And left me like a deflated balloon
Not the love from my twenties
That I thought would last
A lifetime
A marriage
That spiraled to disaster

But the love
Of two people
Who had already walked across hot coals
And eggshells
Who survived shredded hearts
And knew
What they wanted from a partner
And what they didn't

And found it

The Smallest Piece

I am reading
Again
Devouring
The books
On my
Nightstand
And from my
Bookshelves

I still have
Moments
Hours
Of thumbing
Through Instagram
Videos
Of you singing
And the
Easy distractions
Of social media

But reading
Requires
A quiet mind
And calm

Maybe
The smallest piece
Of me
Is healing

Eight Months

Eight months
But yesterday it was seven
The day before, six
And, somehow,
Just the other day
We were together

Sigh

Stepping out of the shower
I realize your shampoo
Conditioner
And body wash
Are still on
The shower shelves
Your cologne
In the medicine cabinet
Your slippers
On the floor
The walking stick
You were carving
Stands behind the front door
And your guitars
Hang in the bedroom
The picture of us
At the brewery
Is on the mantel
Beside the urn
With your ashes

How

You were here
And in an instant
Gone
I just don't
Understand

A First Step

I'm going shoe shopping
This morning
With my daughter
We both need something
New
A new shoe
A next step
Spring is here

Day 257

I've started my next project
Cataloguing your lyrics
Pulling together
Every scrap of paper
Every folded piece of napkin
Every little spiral notebook
And Post-It note
That you kept
With words of your passion
Words you knew
Had that spark of life
That would become a song
I touch the pages
I feel you
I didn't know
How deeply we paralleled
In our bits of paper
Mine, the next great novel
Yours, a gold record

Spring

Your daffodils have bloomed
I never noticed
How many you'd planted
Over the years
A few bulbs here
There
And a sea of them
Down the hill
To the garden
A random flower
At the deck stairs
They greeted me
This morning
And I appreciated
Their beauty
And your work
To make your piece of the world
Beautiful

You were my adventure.

Thunder

The first April thunderstorm
Rolled in
I watched
The pouring rain
Smelled the ozone
And felt the
Warm breeze
Through the screen door
The world keeps going
And I feel
So small

Why

I want to cry
I don't want to cry
The tightrope I walk
With unsteady feet

Why am I here
Why is this my reality
As I grow older
And realize the pain
Everyone must face
I just ask
Why

Without you, each day brings an existential crisis.

Ten months

I climb into bed
Shut off the light
Turn onto my side
And feel the pillow against my back
It used to be
Your back
Against mine
Skin to skin
Comforting and close
It used to be

May 1st

Too close to June
The daffodils have come
And gone
And days are warmer
Nights brisk
I have thoughts
Of planting
Flowers
Vegetables
A deck garden
But you
Never leave my thoughts
And how do I
Do this
Without you

Eating Alone

I cooked fish last night
Not like we used to
Over a glass of wine
With fresh lemon
Herbs from the garden
Laughter
This was from a box
Breaded
In a pan
I ate it slowly
Cutting away
The crunchie bits
No one across from me
Only the sound
Of utensils
The silence
Profound

Memories of Spring

The bags of dirt
On the deck
Smell like spring
Seedlings waiting
The excitement
Of a new garden

But all I can see
Are the memories of us
Building chicken wire walls
Around our first garden
"Checking on the plants"
But really snacking
On the yellow cherry tomatoes
Because they were the sweetest
And you reminding me
I promised to weed
We planted onions
For the first time
And reveled
When they came up
Dug potatoes
Marveled at the cucumbers
Beans and squash
Laughing so hard
When you called it *squanch*
Forever a smile
Between us

The bags of dirt
Lean against the pots

. . . but it doesn't feel like spring . . .

Missing You

I stare out the window
Willing you home
Waiting for you
To walk up our steps
I can see you
Baseball cap backwards
Torn jeans
And Umbrella Corp shirt
Hands rough
From working
On someone's deck
Always building
Creating
And so happy to be home

I miss you

I Cried

I cried on Mother's Day
A few tears
Deep sadness
Even though
The sun was shining
On a crisp spring morning
I'd had my coffee
A frittata
Of spinach and egg white
Wished others
A happy day
And smiled
But then I cried
Just a little
And missed you
So much
The little things
You bringing me
A mug of coffee
And snuggling
On the couch
While watching
The news
You picking up
Before the kids
Came by
And happiness
You made
Every day
Right

Your Flag

Memorial Day is coming
I should have plants
Ready and waiting
But all I have
Are pots with old dirt
And sticks
Memories of gardens past
But your flag is flying

Woodchucks

The woodchucks
Have grown bold
And plod up
The deck steps
Roaming
Searching
Trying to get
The few vegetables
And herbs
I potted
My attempt
At a small garden
They must know
You're not here
To chase them
To find chicken wire
And wood
To build barriers
Perhaps they remember
Staring
At the luscious vegetables
Of our prior gardens
Thwarted
With mouths watering
And now feel
Victorious

Day 336

The time
For counting days
Has ended
And a sorrowful countdown
Begins
Four weeks from today
The anniversary
Of your passing
I stare
At the calendar

One year

One year

And I'm not okay
At least the firsts without you
Are nearly over
But then I fear
The seconds

Not a Year

It hasn't been a year
That's an unacceptable
Amount of time
For my mind
To comprehend
It hasn't been a year
It's been a minute
An hour
And yet
It's been
Forever
And I can't
Forgive time
For marching on

Left Behind

I am a rock
Lodged in a river
Water surging past
Like time
Taking no notice
Making barely a ripple
In this thing
Called life

At least I was your ever after.

You were the music.
You were my music.

They say there is a red thread that connects soulmates and transcends death. We were blessed to have found each other in life, and I know you'll be waiting for me on the other side.

Until then, my love.
Until then.

Barb Shadow

.

ABOUT THE AUTHOR

Barb Shadow is a writer, living with her family on the East Coast. While this is her second book of poetry, Barb has also authored a series of horror novels and compiled three anthologies of true ghost stories. When not out investigating the paranormal, she can be found at her writer's desk, coffee in hand, dreaming up nightmares for her readers.

To find out more about Barb and get updates on her upcoming titles, visit **barbshadow.com**. There you can contact her with any comments or questions you have. She is always happy to connect with fans!

Barb can also be found on Facebook **@BarbsWriting** and Instagram at **barbshadowwrites**.